I0776184

What Puts the Smile

on Your Face?

Gary R Kirby

a candle flames the forest

raindrops flood the stream

tiny things can flame or flood us

a single smile can transform us

forward

After finishing *What Puts a Smile on Your Face* five years ago, I thought I had shared enough smiling happiness that I could now sour it a bit with some poetry. But those warm, room lightening smiles kept breaking across my face Gifts unexpected! Out of a habit of asking them for the source of their smiles, I occasionally did so. Because I told some smilers that I might quote them in a second book, guilt piled up.

I was keeping some smilers waiting to see their quotes. So I finally shifted into typing gear-- my least favorable part of writing. I apologize to those whose quotes are missing. I didn't censor any, including language. But my own language cannot match, and has lost a little of the light of your smiles. For a while I gave out some cards with an email address that did not open. If anyone emailed anything to me and they do not find their quotes in this book, if you try again and send to kirbygary1@gmail.com (placing "*Smiles*" in the subject line) that would tweak my conscience enough to start a third volume.

And to these smilers as you read your reasons for smiling at that moment in time, I hope you keep smiling in the knowledge that your smiling and your sharing in this book will put smiles on other faces! And maybe even refresh your own.

To each of you, thank you for your smile!

dedication

To those who shared the secret of the source behind their smiles.

To my wife Midge whose smile and shining eyes first caught me and slayed me. I am not exaggerating. At first sight I dropped a ping-pong paddle on the table and floated over to her. This book contains one of her smiles, but she'll now have to read all of your smiles, and thus smile more, to find hers.

To the smilers close to me! I am especially grateful for who you are, positive loving supportive people who pick me up with your smiles.

And to all the smilers in the world (and I think even the dourest of humans sometimes smiles a little) these smiles are for you!

contents

the smile givers

When approaching a stranger with an astonishing question like: "What puts that smile on your face?" you would expect some unusual reactions. But no one was grumpy, no one gave me a "Mind you own business buddy." Only once out of these many replies I was asked: "Why are you asking me that?" And also only once I received a suspicious stare with a long pause before what I perceived to be an honest answer. And also, only one time I received a negative reason that the person was smiling--you will have to read the book to find it.

What would you do if a smiling intrusive stranger asked you about your smile? By far and away I would receive a positive look such as surprised, happy, or quizzically smiling. Most of the smilers answered readily and spontaneously and often increased the warmth and brilliance of their smiles.

Some of the responders, usually those with the quizzical smiling look, paused, but when I told them I would put their quote in a book, they all shared the reasons or feelings behind their smiles. About 20% of them were surprised enough to need another prompt such as: "Well, what makes you happy?" Then they all answered, some pouring out a list of things.

As I have repeated elsewhere, almost all of the smilers and I departed that quick encounter smiling broader and deeper, and quite often those around who saw the exchange were also smiling. Happiness is...

About the photo on the cover.

My two sisters, Karen and Jean, grace this cover. I am a far better man because I had sisters like them. They both lived helping people. Their vitality, brilliance, goodness, warmth, and smiles fill a lot of us.

the smile catcher

What really puts the smile most on my face? Why a smile of course, and I suspect it does it for you. It's not like a contagious yawn, but it is a friendly active greeting from another human, and sometimes it is an offer to connect.

After a smile I beam brighter, I feel lighter, and the world is better! I am full of gratefulness that such people exist! There are many of them. I hope their liquid sunlight smiles pull the crinkles to the side of your lips.

All of these responders first smiled before I approached them and asked them for the source behind their smiles. There is a disproportion of women over men, because I think women smile more, and because I know I am more attracted to a woman's smile so I would be more likely to inquire from them. So, here's to the smiling ladies! And to the gentlemen who could learn from them!

Because I did not always have my phone or pen handy (and my memory is now as short as an echo) some of the citations may be shaky, some names misspelled (sorry), and even though everyone gave me their first name, at times I failed to record them and have used: "*Anon*" (even more sorry). When the exclamation mark is inside the quotes, it is because of the enthusiasm in the voice.

With those qualifications, these responses are as close to verbatim as I was able to record them. None are fictional.

As you read, imagine the smiling faces that go with their words!

what puts the smile

on your face

§

Near the top of Bald Hill in Oregon's coastal mountains, in a huge deserted skeleton of a barn, a family of four and their daughter's friend draped the timbers in gymnastic maneuvers. Two of them smiled brilliantly, so I asked them the question I would ask all of the smilers you will meet: "What puts the smile on your face?" Clare and Rebecca each gave me the same, one-word answer: "Gymnastics."

§

Rene, I believe was the third girl's name, and she said while hanging upside down: "Playing with my friends."

§

The gymnasts' mother, Emily said: "Just being outside."

§

Brandon, riding a road bike up a hilly, rocky path, paused by us at the top of Bald Hill and told us that his smile came because: "I just got back into town. And being here."

§

A coyote put a smile on Stephan's face this morning. I met Stephan walking in a wetlands before dawn and he was smiling excitedly. "Did you see that coyote?" he enthused.

§

Kat working beside Steve, said: "Having a good job and a good work environment." As Kat was replying, Steve puffed up his chest and pointed to himself as the "good work environment."

§

Andi, a check-out worker in Market of Choice in Corvallis Oregon said: "God. And I'm in love."

§

Lils, a young waitress in a rural country restaurant handled customers like a hostess in a five star restaurant. She said: "Sunshine. And other people's success."

I feel humble when I meet altruistic people like that. She is making the success of this book.

§

The Cruise In Diner, set out in the midst of Oregon farms, is better than a five star because of the stars who serve there, and because of the amazing owner. Terry is an Electro Physiologist who worked 40 years with Stanford professors studying cancer cells through an electronic microscope. Seven years ago he opened his restaurant, and half of his thirty thousand customers participated in his studies of the effect of strictly organic, local foods on diabetes and other metabolic disorders.

Terry sat with me while I ate and talked fast covering the science and the food remedies. To my knowledge Terry was solid on his facts. He said he was serving food and knowledge as "payback" for all he had received.

I was so engrossed in listening to him that I almost forgot to ask him about the source of his smile. And the answer as expected: "Giving back to others."

§

Terry's wife, Nancy, really had the smile but I lost the reason that I had written down. Hopefully a temporary loss, because I will return for more than a lunch.

§

Emanuelle working at WinCo, one of the largest food stores of them all, said "You've gotta have it." He had a couple of half dimples that fitted nicely into the half crinkled sides of his top lip as if to say--that is the way the game is played.

§

Michelle was on a high this Saturday morning. I said you had a really good night last night. She replied, with a twinkle, "My husband is good some days."

§

Cailey, appearing too young for her response, said: "My son." then she added, "This weather."

§

Steve in UPS says" I don't even have to think: my granddaughter."

§

Sherry, and I forget where I met her, said: "My job, my health--just the basics. And I have a house."

§

Anon: "Phone. Family." That was the first *phone* response I received, but considering its epidemic spread, I expect others.

§

[The following interchange is longer than most, but it is worth reading to the amazing inspirational end to find the incredibly motivating force behind this smile!]

Ellie, with a small boy of about two said: "Everything. It's all perfect."

I questioned this absolute idealism and asked her what else was perfect.

She responded: "The day, my son Theo, my husband--everything."

I asked her if she was perfect too.

She answered: "Yes," and gave me another aware smile as if to show she knew that she had made a bold statement that could appear to be egotistic.

I cautiously asked her what her philosophy behind that perfection was, and she said: "Well, you will think it is kind of strange..." as she paused.

>

\>

"Now I'm really interested!"

"It's counterintuitive "

"I'm starting to like the way you think."

"I expect everything to go the worst possible way, and even if it is bad, then it is not as bad as I imagined!"

"No one has ever said that to me before!" I told her. "Thomas Carlyle, a Victorian writer, said something similar, but he did not go that far. He said 'Make your claim of wages a zero,' and then everything after that is an infinite gift. [I think I was adding to that quote somewhat]. Your wisdom starts further back in the negative column: Carlyle only started at zero."

Then she explained the deep source of her thinking. She said: "I have a chronic disease that has helped me to think positively."

"Wow. Would you send me some of that in writing."

"Sure," she said as she walked away and smiled again.

I said: "You <u>are</u> perfect."

§

Ezzi, a brand new middle school principal from New Orleans, was puffing near the top of Mt. Evans in Colorado. He was not going to reach the summit. He had come from sea level on that day, so his exhaustion was understandable. He said his smile came from the amazing world around him: this was his first time in the mountain. His smile also came from within: he explained his solid philosophy of education that placed the responsibility on the person at the top of an organization to set the mood and the pattern and the model. He was going to be that model.

Ezzi was so exhilarated by his first mountain that the said he would try to bring all the students "here" by their fifth grade.

§

Lisa with her family in a hair-cutting salon: "Our 158 acres and my family." Her boys were impressive, and the acreage had its appeal.

§

Anna and Jonathan from B C Victoria are standing
on Hurricane Hill in the Olympic Peninsula
overlooking the valley towards Hurricane Ridge.
They are one of the more positive couples I have
met. Jonathan had so many reasons for smiling that
he promised to send me a list. Anna said: "How
can you not smile with all this?

§

Tammy gave me the best haircut I've had in
Oregon. I asked her how she did it and she said: "I
listen to my customers and give them what they
ask for." But about what makes her smile: "When I
get to go to Hawaii. I smile when I go to bed, and
when I get up, because it's better for you. It seems
to put you in good spirits. And I always call my
daughter."

§

Teeya, hiking the Oregon Coast Trail, said: "I'm just a happy person."

§

And Jonathan said he kept a mantra going in his head which said: "Stay Awesome."

§

Anon. A walker towards Myrtle Falls on Mt. Rainier gave one word: "Flowers!"

§

Massimo said he smiles because he's a Maltese Pisano. I guess he means that they are happy people.

§

Ranger Joe, talking to another visitor at Mt. Rainier Lodge, drew me to him by flashing a George Clooney smile. As I stood in front of the lodge looking at the massive, glacier covered mountain I asked Ranger Joe where was the highest path we could take with the least snow.

He looked at me as his eye glinted and I saw it coming: "Arizona." We laughed and laughed--his smile which started it all, rolled into mountain laughter.

§

Lloyd and Joyce sat on the deck at Mt. Rainier. Lloyd's smile matched his white beard and hair, and he wore a shirt with "Body Armour" on it. Since he looked amazingly fit I said, "The shirt matches the man."

Lloyd quickly replied patting his stomach: "You can't see what's down here."

§

A smile almost always gets a smile, and a great smile can strike and transform the other. I walked into the post office and I was almost instantly in love with Kari. Normally I would not put that in a book that my wife reads, but sharing it here it would show the power of a smile! Kari just looked so warm and wonderful sitting there smiling. As we talked, we realized that I had already gotten her smile probably three years ago. But I am repeating her again, because she is worth a double entry and a lot more. Somewhere in the first book of Smiles, there is a quote that recorded what put the smile on her face back then, and it certainly works now!

§

In a former automobile showroom that sat vacant for 30 years, I found a lot of smiles: Jessica working in a confectionary said, "I have it on every day." I asked her what else put it there and she said, naturally, "Working with chocolate in Denver's amazing Central Market."

§

Lindsey, making chocolate candies also in the Central Market (yes, there was more than one chocolate shop!) said: "People like you. Good stuff. My dog. My family."

I am touting the smiles in this book, not the places, but places can boost the wattage of the smiles. Often such places are in nature, but here they were in the city, in a place like this which was wide-open, artistically arranged, with those chocolate shops, ice cream parlors, bakeries, coffee bars, wine bars, a booze bar, butcher shops, fish-shops, and a glowing pizza furnace surfaced with mosaic tiles.

§

Buyi from South Africa: "The Lord." When I asked her which denomination she said: "I'm Christian."

§

Kate in the Lake Crescent Lodge in the Olympic National Park said: "It's my birthday today!"

§

Hiking the alpine walks up Mt. Rainier bursting gloriously with flowers below the brilliant snowfields under that massive mother mountain of many glaciers, Susan said: "Flowers and mountains!"

Her husband Jeff came over and she quickly added: "Oh yes, he's put the smile on my face for twenty years."

§

"Has it been that long?" queried Jeff. "I thought we were just married last year."

§

"Helping everyone out. Fishing--it's relaxing," said Matthew.

§

Muriel, up in the alpine meadows of Mt. Rainier gave me an overflowing good morning greeting while passing. When I asked her: "It's so beautiful! How could you not be smiling?"

§

Laura, and her lovely daughter Olivia, from New Orleans, were walking part of the Oregon Coastal Trail. They were smiling and they promised to send me their smiling pictures and the reasons they smiled. They didn't, probably lost in the wonder of the Oregon Coast. Others also have promised, so if you happen to read this Laura, it is not too late.

§

At the summit of Mt. Evans in Colorado, Siena and Brad were breathing in the view. Siena responded with a query: "Right now?" And then sweeping her arm around to the view of the mountain ranges said: "This!" Then as she nodded towards Brad she added: "And at other times, him."

§

Brad stood beside her looking down at Summit Lake and said, "Fishing." Then he quickly added "Siena." And possibly to cover his embarrassment with humor he said: "And right now the view is good. And good food."

§

Anon: "I like to smile at my customers. I think it makes people happy and I hope it makes a better day for them."

§

Katie, coming up from a promontory jutting out into Pacific Ocean and overlooking the devil's cauldron, said: "Only one?" She also promised to send me many things that made her smile because: "One is just not enough."

§

Raven, dark-haired and well named with just the friendliest good morning freshest smile, told me when I asked: "Morning sunshine!"

"Anything else?

"That's it."

I knew there was a lot more behind that smile, but I was not going to press her because being a teller in a bank is not exactly the place where you wax eloquent about happiness and smiles. Sad thing about money that way.

§

Molly in Colorado said: "People! I wish I could describe them all to you. Thank you."

§

Zack was at the checkout counter at Barnes and Noble's which had just opened on a Sunday morning. His hair was disheveled and he looked sleepy. I handed him a book, he smiled. "What puts a smile on your face so early this morning?" He replied: "I have to."

That was a beautifully honest reply. Assessing their answers, I have doubted no one of being phony. Many people have been surprised, perhaps nervous, stunned, and with many other emotional responses to a stranger asking that question. Consequently some responses were stilted, but none that I judged fake.

§

Meet Terran. She told me her name was that of the Gaelic God of thunder, whose name in Sanskrit means *water*. Her mother gave her that dual meaning because she is Indian (hence Sanskrit) and they lived in Ireland for quite a while. She appropriately goes by the nickname Tara, the hill of the Great Irish Kings. It is clear that her culture has certainly overlaid her genetic origins with her Irish smile and charm.

§

Cheryl, standing on the top of Mt. Evans in Colorado said: "How can you not smile coming to a place like this?" She said she would email me something about a little man that went around town smiling all the time. Sadly no email came, so the little smiling man will have to run around in our imaginations. Picture him.

§

Up on Mt. Evans, Matilda said: "My life! It's perfect!" And she added that all of her family smiled. A home full of smiles. What a place to grow in, and to have inside herself to boost her up to the mountain top.

§

Olivia, in the Tattered Cover bookstore in Denver, said: "My animals. Especially my chinchillas. And when I'm waking up in the morning and my boyfriend is kissing me."

Wow. And is that boyfriend lucky to be kissing that smile!

§

Steven said that he was starting vacation that night and added that: "I have good kids."

§

Jim at the giant Century Theater in Sacramento California: "Being here and I'm having a great day."

§

This one is dedicated to my daughter Becky: normally she gets quite concerned when I approach strangers and ask them what puts a smile on your face. At that point she likes to get far away from me. In her words I disturb people.

Today Becky made my day! I caught her coming down the entrance corridor of the theater as I was going up. I stopped her and said: "Excuse me M'am, what puts that smile on your face?" Expecting her quick put-down, she turned and gave me a beautiful smile, and a hug, and a kiss, and said, "You!"

Wow! That was worth the whole book and will keep a smile on my face for the whole year, and light my memory when I re-walk that aisle!

§

I'm sitting next to a gentleman and lady in Century Theatre waiting for Wonder Woman to start. I asked the gentleman, and like only a dozen wise men interviewed in this book, he said: "She does!" I told him that's going to make a good night for him.

Returning his tactful answer she said: "Him." She was Jennifer, but I missed his name.

§

David, working at a Peets Coffee in Sacramento, said: "Road Motorcycling is first, then hiking, then summiting, especially at the top with a 360."

§

Brian, the Special Collections Librarian in Denver Central Library: "When I think of my kids."

§

Laura, a smiling librarian in a building with six million volumes, and no readers that I could see, (a commentary on society) sat at her desk in front of an impressive mural and responded surprisingly: "I raise service dogs for the physically disabled."

Expecting some such answer as "books," I have found that I cannot predict the wonderful variety of individual forces and feelings behind the smiles. There are so many creative new responses from people, each one with a different smile, each smile refreshing, lightening, inspiriting, and joyful.

§

Brenda, somewhere in the U.S. but probably not the Southwest, said: "Sunshine."

§

Sarah said: "Life! My kiddos. My husband. Summer time in Oregon."

§

Garrett said: "It's another nice day, hopefully."
He's in Corvallis at a stunning new coffee house
built over a former fast oil change garage. It's the
second such shop in Corvallis, *Tried and True*, and
its coffee is petrol free but still high octane! And a
little-known fact--the light roast has a higher
caffeine content than the dark roast! Check it out.

§

Lynne: "When my dog lies on the bed and wiggles
his tail 'cause he is so happy to see me."

§

Aaron: "Sunshine. And it never hurts to smile.
Coffee helps."

§

"Having your children happy." Now that's a mother, from Roberta.

Her friend, Margie' agrees with her, and she was laughing like she was going to reveal something embarrassing that also made Roberta smile. Instead she reconsidered and said that she was a teacher, and she smiled as she said: "When you can see the moment a student learns something in their life, and their life path goes on."

I think a lot of teachers will feel joy in that expression.

§

Jesus was the name on his badge. He was running customer service in a large discount store. He said he had learned to smile for his job, but that now it was just a natural part of him. One or two other smilers have made the connection that smiling on the outside can change the inside.

§

Meet Deqa who has the kind of smile that makes you feel like you are in love instantly. I walked into a medical care facility inquiring about their coverage, and from afar I was greeted with such a beam I went right over to her. She said, "When people are sick they need a nice smile."

§

Anne-Marie is right! She said, "Sunshine and good news," and the good news that she had just received that morning was that of a baby born! Then she added: "The Rolling Stones."

§

Mark exited a door onto the sidewalk in
Sacramento California, and we almost bumped
into each other. He had such a wide smile as he
was walking away I called out the question to him.
He said: "It's delicious," as he pointed to the sign
over the building: Curry's Club Indian Bistro. He
said: "Best food in town!"

§

Katie, a check-out clerk at the legendary Fred
Meyers in Oregon, said: "Thank you. A lot of
things, personally. I like making other people
smile. And I like art."

§

Megan: "Dancing."

§

Jen was wheeling a suitcase about three miles to her home near the MAX (the light rail) in Portland, Oregon. I had wheeled luggage once a shorter distance, and it was burdensome. I stopped and asked if she wanted a ride. She accepted, and I could hardly lift her suitcase--it was packed with food. She wanted a ride home because her car's brakes had failed. I gave her the name of a good, less expensive mechanic, and then drove her three miles (she was pulling all that weight on those little wheels that far). When I asked her about her smile, she said one word: "Beauty."

Beauty! That was my reward for helping her. I don't recall anyone else saying that so simply. It struck me because "beauty" inspires and drives about eleven volumes of my poetry. Beauty! Wow! Where is another stranger carrying beauty inside who needs a ride?

§

Give up a high tech, high paying job to work in a sports store? Being an engineer was too stressful for Shirley, and now she is selling me a solar lantern that I don't really need. Her husband remains an engineer making the big bucks so she can enjoy working with less stress. She was smiling gorgeously when she said: "I wake up in the morning and see my rose garden and I am happy."

§

Adam was developing photos in an Office Depot. He bristled a mohawk. When I was younger that was the sign of a tough guy (picture Mr. T from the A Team). I didn't expect his helpfulness and his smile. His response: "My kiddo. He's six. And helping people. I always get a joy helping people."

When I asked him how he became that way he said: "I was born with it." While I was hoping for a theory of living that made him happy, I was quite satisfied that nature birthed people like him.

§

Curtis Haley, 29 and from Beaverton Oregon, was running for state senate. He said: "Positive people." That is the core of his campaign, judging from his email: makepoliticspositive@gmail.com, and from his smile.

§

Emily was in Beaverton Oregon's awesome Saturday Market and she offered this spiritual source: "I truly believe God is good and we are blessed, and to be a blessing to others." I was blessed by her smile.

§

Jean, working at the Audubon Society of Portland, said: "Anything! As long as it's not something bad. I like talking to people. I think that's why I said 'anything' as long as it's not tragic."

§

Mark owns the *Evolve* landscaping company. He said "Just taking care of things. Making things beautiful."

§

The lady taking care of Audubon said: "I'm a character and that makes me happy." Then she looked at me and said: "I know a boy with a great face and a great white beard." I was guessing at her meaning, but it did show she was a character.

§

"I had a pretty good day," said Maggie. "I've had a good family, good friends." Maggie has a rolling laughter and a nice smile. Thank you, Maggie.

§

A sunrise smile from the east! A lovely Vietnamese waitress said: "I don't know. I like seeing other people happy. I love my job and I have a good home."

§

Kook and I were talking. Yes, Kook was her Korean name. I told her how it is often used in America, and she smiled. "I believe in Jesus," she said. I asked her what her name meant, and she said *golden flower* and searched for the English name. Finally we came up with Chrysanthemum. Quite appropriate, since *Chrys"* means golden in Greek, and *anthemon* means flower. But in any language she had a golden smile with a spiritual boost.

§

Jen, working for an insurance medical testing company, was behind a window as I walked by. She beamed brightly when I stopped in to ask her. Her response: "Oh, lots of things. Just the joy of being alive. My son! He's eight. That's why I'm so happy to be alive."

It struck me that when children grow up and are single, I doubt if any of them know the joy they gave their parents when they were children. But when they have children, they learn.

§

Gwen, a librarian in Oregon which has the second largest circulation next to New York metropolitan area, said: "When I can actually answer the questions people ask." As a note, I have found librarians to be about the most helpful of all the service sectors.

§

Teresa instantly complimented me as a response to the question: "People like you!"

You can bet that put a bigger smile on my face.

§

Cara said: "It's my thing. I do it all the time. It's better than crying."

§

A beautiful Middle Eastern woman glowed a smile as I walked in the door of an elevator. When I asked her she said, "Being alive!" She said it with such a happy vibrancy that I thought I would write another book called: *What Puts that Lilt in your Voice!* With a smile and a tone of voice like that, I needed no other proof that she was indeed happy "being alive."

§

Trisha, an audiologist, said: "Sunshine and people. The sunshine makes you feel warm and good and so do the people." Insightful analogy merging two warmths!

§

I'm in a library with Serena. Her response was to touch her ring. I naturally thought she was recently engaged or married until she said: "I've been married 30 years." Then she added: "My kids, and laughter, and communication. You have to have communication in this job."

Serena was such a sweetie that I wanted to hug her, but decided not. She must have read my body language because she hugged me and said: "You made my day!" Who made whose day?

§

Mattie said: "Happy people. I'm one of those half-full people."

§

Sharon said: "That's just the way you have to tackle life." And then she said: "You have beauty in every day." Then seeming to know that she had given some deep responses, she smiled to lighten the moment and added: "Jewelry."

§

Julianne, at Fed Express: "The sun! My bunnies. And I've got my granddaughter, Clementine! Born last night at 5:38!"

§

Her smile caught me in the parking lot: "Gosh! I
don't know. So much. You know that saying--'I'm
too blessed to be stressed.'" I didn't get her name,
but I too am blessed by her smile.

§

Shawna greeted me with such a great smile when I
walked into the doctor's office that I said: "Your
smile has already cured me." When I asked her the
question she replied: "I just love this job. I love
coming to work every day, and I think I make a
difference in peoples' lives."
      She made a difference that day in mine, and
I can still see her smile

§

Tiffany on the beach with her child, Zoe. "Life!"
And of course she said, "Sunshine and oceans."

§

"It's sunshine! And my baby. My baby's smile."
said Christine. She told me she had just got here
from Germany. She used to live here and then she
said: "And we bought a new house, and we have a
new car." Sounds like a lot of the American
Dream.

§

Nguyen, with a big smile and a big dog, said:
"Sunshine!" You can guess by "sunshine" that she
had experienced Oregon's coastal rains. She added
her "dog," and said he was a Belgian White
Malinois, a rescue dog. That too would help
explain her smile, something that often goes with
people who are empathetic enough to "rescue"
animals. I asked her if there was anything else and
she said: "Good food. Nice people." I thanked
Nguyen.

§

Out on the rugged Pacific Coast, Cheryl, instantly enthusiastically spouted: "How can you not smile coming to a place like this?" She promised to send me a poem from a friend that she had posted on her refrigerator ever since her friend passed away many years ago. She delivered on her promise and her poem:

A smile is quite a funny thing
It wrinkles up your face
And when it's gone you never find
it's secret hiding place
But far more wonderful it is
To see what a smile can do!
You smile at one
she smiles at you
And so one smile makes two!!"

Thanks Cheryl

§

This poem catches the evocative infectiousness of smiling! Much more often than yawning, a smile comes back. Often, when I ask the question, the smiles grow brighter, I beam back, and the surrounding listeners often smile just watching! Smile! It will go on.

§

My notes on Matilda are scrambled, but I think she is the daughter of Cheryl above. Matilda said her life was perfect, and nodding towards her mother she gave one reason: "I've got a mother like that!"

§

Jan, Jamie, and son Lyon were hiking up the Neahkahni Mountain trail, the highest mountain directly on the Oregon coast. They said something to the effect of: Hiking in places like this!

§

Peter is with his son Drew on a beach on the Pacific Ocean. Peter said: "Drew. I sketch images in the sand, and start a contest with him saying: 'I can make you uglier than you can make me ugly.' It's just great!"

I have done that with my grandson who has out-uglied me. Lucky we sketched in the sand.

§

Meredith. "Sunshine."

§

Kevin was vacationing down the Oregon coast with a glowing smile, coming from the state of Washington. When I asked him what puts a smile on his face. He said: "I just got married!" Surprised me, but we understand the smile.

§

I was talking to a happy woman, a teacher, and I was happier when she responded: "Teaching!" Wow! We need more teachers like that who love children and the interaction and challenge of growing their minds.

§

Megan did not respond with a cliché but said: "Listening to other people's passions." Wouldn't we all like to talk to her for a while?

§

"Fort Collins, Colorado," he said. "But I don't get there often enough. And sunsets! And here, it's gorgeous!"

§

I'm at a tulip farm that rivals pictures of Holland.
I'm talking to Ken Fritt, a photographer from north
of Seattle. Taking pictures makes him happy, but
especially when he goes somewhere and comes
close to capturing the photo he was after. "Seeing
my wife is the most precious, important thing I
could see." And spending time with his kid and his
grandkids is high on his list.

§

It was a week before Christmas. I asked Deanna, a
happy optician in Oregon and she said without any
hesitation: "Chocolate. Holidays. People." And
then she burst out: "I love love love this time of the
year!"

§

Anon. "Having a good day."

§

I was walking down a line of tents with crafts for sale, checking out those that caught my eye when I saw Pete smile. I was drawn into his booth solely for the smile and do not remember what the crafts for sale were. Pete said: "Pretty little girls with rubber boots and cute little dresses." Outside the tent just such a girl was playing who had caught his eye. Pete lived on the Columbia River and I'm sure salmon made him smile for he was concerned how pollution was killing his salmon, and how over-regulation was allowing the seals to proliferate and they ate too many salmon.

§

Patty sat in the tent with him, smiling at Pete's company. She picked up on the little girl theme, and said she had been the parent of three daughters, and remembered them as little girls and said: "How could that not make you smile?"

§

It happened. I almost always get a greeting and a smile when walking the wetland near my home, but the bull-like figure walked by me in a black coat with a hat pulled down over his head, his earphones barely showing. His glum face disappeared into his neck as thick as a football guard. No way to get a smile from that guy. He was thirty feet off to my side, so I did not even attempt a hello.

Later I passed him again as he picked up a plastic bottle littering the path and crushed it. I gave him a thumbs up and wondered if I had badly misjudged him from his clothes and body language.

A third time I was passing him, and now brave enough to interrupt him, I thanked him for his bottle picking up. He broke into a huge smile. His name was Craig. I forgot to ask him the question, but we can guess that helping keep our world in its natural unpolluted beauty, and an appreciation from others, put the smile on his face.

§

Let me bring this floating, smiling trip back to earth. Usually when passing a single walker in the woods, there is always a friendly greeting and a smile. Craig was an exception, but another time a walker was looking into his I-Phone and I did not even get a nod back. What does that say for technology? Or for my rudeness to even nod to a passing woods' walker?

§

Cody the floor supervisor at Best Buy, with a cheery energetic disposition, and who was continuously smiling said: "I like this job." I called for a response as he walked away fast before I had a time to get his answer, but I suspected the source of his smile came from a far deeper place than customer politeness.

§

Danielle said it was a pretty day, even though it
was raining

§

Let's hear it for the pets: Chloe in Beaverton
OR simply said: "Dogs."
And a statistic to the smiling dog owners,
there are slightly more cats as pets. Not too fast cat
owners: more households have dogs. And before
you both start frowning at each other and losing
those pet-generated smiles, fresh water fish surpass
both of them in numbers.
Anyone got a gecko?

§

Anon. Waiting for a replacement for her defective
airbag in her Honda: "Cats. I wake in the morning
and they give me smiles."

§

Barbara, volunteering in a small school of only 18 students on the wild Pacific coast quickly listed three words: "Kids. Reading. Nature."

§

A short lady dressed in purple walking a little dog passed me several times on the circuit through Orchard Park. Each time she was smiling, but not at me; so when I stopped her and asked her she said I'm listening to a funny podcast. I missed her name, and sheepishly again state: Anon.

§

Vivian, in the High Road Art Gallery in Truchas NM said: "God. Then you guys."

§

I met Liz walking around a pond where the geese covered the waters. She sent me this email:

> I looked you up online and saw your pic on Amazon along with the list of your books. Impressive-it made me smile. Here are a few things that make me smile:
>
> My husband's effort to make me laugh every day
>
> The opportunity to affect a complete stranger's day with the simple act of sharing a smile
>
> My black lab's gray eyebrows giving her face even more expression than before
>
> My 6-month-old granddaughter's smile that causes her to light up like a candle
>

>

When my forsythia blooms telling me it's
officially spring

When I take time to consider the
wonderful quality of friends I have acquired

Seeing my adult children being friends with
each other

Life is full of joy if you take time to look for
it and appreciate the simple things around
you

I hope this is helpful, because being helpful
generally makes me smile as well

Liz

Liz! I will probably never meet you again, but each
item on that list warmed me! Most of them have
made me smile also. I hope your sharing them here
repays your effort as your smiles ripple across the
world.

§

Christina, after a short discussion referring to my friend John and me, said: "You two, being genuine and caring."

§

Jennifer, on a walk by the library: "That's the joy of my Lord in my heart." As she said it she smiled even more beautifully. If I meet many more such smiles, I would wonder whether a second baptism would wash away my frowns.

§

"I am just a joyous person. I like to smile when I say something. I like to see the positive in every day!" I encouraged her to go on: "You're on a roll!" She was laughing and smiling say right here there's so much around us to be thankful for. She poured out smile starters so fast I did not record them. The first name of this vibrant smiling laughing woman sounded like "Leslie." Sorry to whomever. If you read this and correct me, I will correct your name.

§

Elise: Helping hurt animals.

§

Working at a Dollar Store and smiling,
Amber said: "Everything!" By her
brightness she meant it.

§

Allison in a Patagonia store: "Being in nature."

§

I was with a friend jostling each other as we were
going into a Peets Coffee shop. A couple were
beaming on a bench outside the door, perhaps
watching us. I asked the woman and she
responded: "You, lovely people! " I thanked her
and asked: "Anything else?" "My Mother. I
inherited her genes, and maybe her smile."

§

A tall blonde woman was walking in the rain on Hug Beach on the Pacific Ocean. A small dog followed her. She gave me a smile so I popped the question. She just smiled more brightly and kept walking. I called to her: "Hey! I'm serious. I write books. I'll put that smile inside of one of them."

She replied: "It's a beautiful day." It was raining, but she was right. At the beach it's always a beautiful day, and by extension the same could be said of most days and most places. Since she was walking away I did not yell and ask her for her name.

She becomes one of those many people who have touched me, like others who have touched you, with the kindness of their glances and smiles, and who never pass our way again, but have left that touch of themselves in us. Thank you, nameless lady!

§

A handsome young couple sporting high-tech clothes, sat in front of a coffee shop. They smiled at my four-year-old grandson. Ally quickly responded: "Fresh air, trees, ocean. There's nothing more peaceful than nature."

§

Sitting next to Ally is Bobby, and even though he has had a lot of time to think of a response, he said what first came to his mind: "Sitting on the bench with my girl."

§

He said it so warmly that I dropped on the bench opposite them and said: "That one made me sit down."

§

Susan, who was stacking twenty-pound boxes of frozen salmon, said, expectedly: "I love fishing, and the beautiful views."

§

A gentleman certifiably talented by his last name, Kirby, was carving a horse head for a carousel. When I asked him what puts that smile on his face he said: "I love coming here: the fellowship of the carvers, the enthusiasm of the children." Kirby is carving a carousel piece in a room full of carvers. Judging from what they have accomplished I think they're going to create probably the loveliest carousel on earth. Also he said he learned something every day and that kept him smiling. Kirby retired from being a mechanical service technician to the much more artistic tangible touch of wood.

To understand what is going on doing this passé craft, please read the next entry.

§

This is Jack running this incredible historic carousel museum in Albany, Oregon with twenty or so volunteer carvers. They've been at it for twelve years. Jack said: "I just enjoy getting up every day." His smile was real and spread into his laughing.

Since I recorded the two gentlemen above, the carousel has opened! It is glorious after their twelve years of artistic endeavor. If you ever reach Oregon add this stop to the mountains, the gorge, and the ocean.

§

Kathy: "I don't know." She laughed. "The sunshine outside? But the hailstorm was nice yesterday." Since both kinds of weather were welcome in Oregon, I would guess the smile came not from the outside but from the inside.

§

When I can, I walk on the dirt paths in the woods but crossing the asphalt path for walkers and bikers. I burst out of the woods close to a walker on the asphalt path. To not scare her, I quickly explained that the woods were easier on my knees. She just smiled easily and began talking. I asked her the smile question and got an unusual response as she said: "I am a light holder. I hold some of the positive forces for the planet, and that puts a smile on my face. And I'll tell you, I came through a lot of adversity in my life and knowing that God walks with me and through me. I have walked through hell and now I get to experience heaven." As she spoke with a smile in her voice, she pulled heaven from her head and it radiated out.

Sometimes we might want to negatively categorize someone who says: "I am a light holder." Regardless of its source, I would welcome some of that brightness that glows the face of Karen, the light holder.

§

Meet Evie, one of the friendliest southwesterners I have met. She said: "There's not much I do that doesn't put a smile on my face. I'll tell you what else gets a smile on my face: pizza. I freaking love pizza. My husband doesn't, so I order it out on the road. Who doesn't like pizza?"

§

At a stop on the highway to the sea, she stood behind the counter with a long 50 caliber gun mounted on the wall behind her. She said: "Leaving now." Her shift was done. Then she added: "Guns. I get excited about putting together a basic assembly and a 50-bolt carrier group." With her personality I am sure that that long gun will not be used to hurt anyone.

§

"It's just a lovely day!" I wish I could show you the face behind those words, a face more lovely than the day, of this young mother with a gentle kind smile holding a little girl about two. Maggie is the name of the Madonna, and the little girl is lucky!

§

Anon: "It's a good day, it's a beautiful day, I like my world, and I'm remodeling some houses." This guy with a great smile is a happy guy standing next to me in a line at Subway.

§

Anon offered some wisdom that rhymed: "You get what you get, and you don't throw a fit. You've got a life. Live with it."

§

Adebabay, (yes the spelling is correct) working at a McDonald's in Denver appeared to be from Jamaica and was still learning English. She was smiling and giggling trying to figure out what I was all about asking her about smiles. Finally she said: "Job."

§

Tony, in the Denver airport, said, "Not being late for work." I asked her if this happened often, and she said: "I had to go upstairs and twist and turn all around and come down here and I wasn't sure where I was going." That was when she explained it was her first day struggling through employee security and very happy to be working. Being on time the first day is smile time.

§

To take a break from all these sanguine silly smiling people, for the first time I got the response: "Not much." Then Duane smiled again after he said it, but it was a sad sweet smile, and I read that he was unhappy. When I asked him if there was anything else he repeated, "Not much. That's about it."

He was now smiling a little brighter though, and not out of a social sense of politeness. My asking him seemed to cheer him up a little, judging by his face and voice.

Duane remains the only person who has responded in a weak neutral tone, probably a little on the negative side.

§

Jaenada, in New Mexico near Taos: "Sunshine. Children. And flowers."

§

Anita wore a doctor's mask but I could see the smile crinkle her eyes above her mask. I wanted to see the rest of her smile, but she was contagious, she said, from her flu shot. She said: "We have to earn those wrinkles."

§

Rebecca instantly responded: "Number one, God. Number two, I find that if you keep a positive attitude it really helps your day go better."

§

Oleaviar, one of the quickest, friendliest check-out clerks ever at WinCo, a giant of a food store, listed: "Babies. Cookies. Pound Cake. And babies again. And then puppies."

§

I'm in *Violet's Sweet Treats* (ice cream!) speaking with Colleen, and I asked her what puts a smile on her face She said, "Working here with my daughter," as she patted her daughter on the back. Her daughter's name was Violet.

§

And the namesake of the Sweet Shop, Violet, said, "Helping people."

§

"Joy shines in your smiles, and smiling sends joy to your eyes." Darned if I know who said that. The quote is so beautifully poetic I googled it. I did not find the creator, so one of the unnamed smilers gave us a wonderful image of the connectedness of joy/smiles/shining eyes! Thank you!

§

Allise, brewing coffee in the Insomnia
Coffee Shop on the Oregon beach said: "Oh man.
I'd say good friends. Animals. My dogs. I love
people, all different kinds."

Her smile still stands out among the many
great, human smiles that have filled me. I easily
see her happy face as I recall and write this.

§

Kelsey, also serving java, simply said: "Animals."

§

Derrick, at a Valvoline Oil Change: "I woke up
this morning. Somewhere on this earth someone
didn't wake up."

§

Mo: "I usually smile, and if you greet people with a smile you usually get one right back. I'm thinking of all the things I'm grateful for. [Now she is really smiling as she recalls!] My husband, my kids, and you too."

"And me too?" I questioned back, and now I was really smiling to.

"And you too," she replied glowing as she gave me an exotic raspberry chocolate bar that she was able to give to special customers. I had just received my first bribe or reward ever, after asking over 1000 people. I dislike clichés, but maybe it pays to smile.

§

Susie came up to the coffee shop riding a high-tech bike. She showed me that it charged her computer and she punched something in her pocket to lock it. When I gave her the smile question she smiled quite lively and said pointing to her bike: "That" puts a smile on my face."

§

Stephanie, walking along a path said: "Cheerful people." Then she added that it was really all humans, just being human.

And speaking of being human, Stephanie was a young Brit with such a lovely smile, that I flirted with her saying: "If I weren't so old and so married, I would just hustle you."

She laughed and said her hound would protect her, and she pointed to Nigel, a pup who was named after her dad, who had not wanted her to get a dog. So she called it "Little Nigel, and now he loves it!"

§

Jackie with a huge smile said: "I'm retiring at the end of this month, on the 29th!" And then she added, "And I do love this job."

She was a happy person while she was working, and she's happy going out. What a way to work happy, retire, and live!

§

Tim, white beard, white teeth, limping from an old sports injury, smiled as he limped by. So I asked him: "Just enjoying life, keeping up with my friends and my relationships."

§

"It beats the alternative" said Karen, a lovely lady, sandy brown hair, sitting here with me waiting for an oil change. When I asked her for more things that made her smile, her answer: "Being an ICU nurse makes you appreciate the simple things." Wow. A profound statement. Critical life situations make you realize that basic things, like people, like life, are most important.

§

The sun was out, and people were circling the park. Yukti said her smiles came from her Bernese Mountain Dog.

§

When I asked Casha, who was selling me a cup of coffee, what her name meant, surprisingly she wouldn't tell me even though she appeared open and spontaneous in her smiling. She admitted Casha was not her real name but her cashiering name. Although she would not tell me her real name, (Hey, when a weirdo out of the blue asks you about your smile, you might not want to give them your name) yet she answered my question: "What puts that lovely smile on your face?" She responded "You." Of course I totally believed her answer.

§

Chad at Valvoline said: "Getting my son tonight!" And then, I guess he was a little self-conscious about his smile because he added: "Usually I don't smile because I have a broken tooth."

From my experience, all faces become more beautiful and attractive when graced with a smile.

§

At Madison Wisconsin, inside the largest U-Haul I have ever seen, probably because of the huge number of University students continually changing apartments, Jamie, a young man, blushed when I asked him. And his coworker right away chuckled loudly as if to say: "I know why he's smiling." Then Jamie told me, but I have to cover his reason and respect his confiding.

§

This is not a paid advertisement. The next several quotations come from the same establishment full of smilers. I have just experienced my best overnight hotel stay at Larkspur Landing, in Sacramento California. It's about $149 a night but they have free coffee all hours, free tea, free amenities for your pets if you have them, free washing machines, free breakfast-- but of course this is not about amenities. The primary gift they give is their warmth and their smiles.

§

When I walked in Larkspur there was
Amber. She glowed warm and nurturing at the
counter; a fire was flickering in a living room
adding to the atmosphere. Amber pointed to her
resident soft gray cat, but when I asked her she
responded: "Dogs."
      "Anything else?" I asked. She replied: "You
may think this is funny, but grumpy old men."
      "Are you insulting me?"
She smiled and said: "When they walk up they
don't even need to say anything, and I can tell if
they're grumpy. But I always get them smiling."

§

Back to the amenities at Larkspur: This is the first
hotel room I have been in that also has a recycling
waste paper basket in each guest room. But then,
this is California.

§

Then I met the manager of Larkspur: Shawn, a man with a lot of gusto and a big warm smile, who later told me he is moving up to become regional manager of five of these facilities, and then he hopes to be general manager of all of them, and then start his own chain. He responded to my smile question: "I love my job. I love my team. I'm here more than I'm with my family. And we treat everyone like family, and we treat our employees and each other like a family. I tell them to greet each new person walking in as if they are a close friend that they haven't seen for five years. It always works."

§

Since Shawn was so successful I kiddingly encouraged him to take charge of the old folks' facilities in our country so I could be happy in one of them. I said: "How would you solve our problem of how we manage our aging population

>

>

in some of our retirement, and assisted living, and long-term facilities?

His response was uplifting: "You want to make them happy. You want to make them want to stay. Give them a lot of fun. A lot of games, a lot of parties, a lot of exciting stuff. You give them as much to do as they want. Make it a happy place."

§

The second day I continued probing to see if the happy place was real, and if all the employees beamed with the smiling spirit. I walked up to Gabriella at the desk who was working on her computer, but instantly she gave me a smile and full attention. I said: "That was a nice smile, what put that on your face?" She replied "Honestly, just sometimes if I see a guest I give them a smile."

I replied, "Now that's your expected hotel comment, what makes you smile at other times when you're not here?" Her reply was: "Just looking at nature. "

Wow nature! That makes me smile inside and outside and feel at home. Gabriella, we are both children of nature. I smiled a lot during my stay at Larkspur.

§

Andrea: "Just being alive makes me smile!"

§

Noemi: "Humor does, all the time--it gets to me."

§

Julie: "I'm too much of a thinker. Watching little kids. They're amazing."

§

"Helping People," said Teresa.

§

Griselda: "I like...how to express...my English is...I think I want to make the customer feel happy."

§

Jen, a receptionist at Kaiser, said "Putting the smile on somebody else's face."

§

Anon: "Prozac! And its Merry Christmas time."

§

Kris: "Just thankful to be alive."

§

Evie, working at Best Buy: "My grandkids. Customers who are nice. Being alive!" I wish I could record Evie's laughter for you.

§

Sierra: "Coffee. And I'm off at 11:30 and I have tomorrow off!" Sierra said this with such enthusiasm that one would think she really hated her work. Luckily Alison popped around the corner and said: "She just turned 21."

Now we know why the next day off was so important.

§

Jamie, a graphic artist who designed a sign for me: "Seeing people I love being happy."

§

Rolanda working at Loews: "Being retired, and this is a fun job."

§

Jean, a cardiologist: "My four grandchildren."

§

Laura: "You know what? A happy person. Kindness."

§

Sherry: "I just love being around people! I'm just thankful for just what I have." (Apology for the editorial here, but I think she is onto the secret of happiness from which smiles spring.)

§

At Big 5 Sports, Diana said: "The people I work with."

§

Kerri, also at Big 5 said: "Diana puts a smile on my face."

§

Jeff: "Wine."

§

Stu: "Nice weather."

§

Jerry, being near the Yaquina Light House on the Oregon coast said: "Just being here."

§

Alison, in one of Oregon's green medical dispensaries, otherwise called a pot store, said: "Sunshine! Animals!"

§

Andriana: "Just talking to customers."

§

Elisha: "I don't know. I enjoy the simple pleasures
in life. Almost anything. Seeing someone smile.
And butter. And Sunshine, Oh Yes!"

§

Anon: "You just do it day by day. No epiphany
will fix your life, but inch by inch and day by day
you smile."

§

Lisa in Office Max: "It's a god-given gift. I was
born with it. The company told me my smile is a
million-dollar asset for them. I am a million-dollar
person! I was adopted. My step mom was crabby. I
didn't want to be like that."

§

Referring to the preceding quote, I have deliberately started a new paragraph so as to not detract from it. It is wise. A re-read shows what choice can effect in our lives. Also, aren't many of us wondering whether Lisa is making much more than minimum wage, even with that million-dollar smile?

§

Amy, hiking down one of Oregon's capes: "Just being alive."

§

Emma, a Geek at Best Buy: "My fiancé. He just enlisted. I have known him for twelve years."

§

Sherry: "The first thing that comes to mind... I have a second chance at life! I was ill, a tumor, and I am going to live life! I sky dived."

§

Casey: "When you get that awake moment from a good cup of coffee."

§

Nicole, a receptionist at Kaiser: "Nice people. Colorful flowers."

§

Stephanie: "Spending time with friends and family."

§

I was talking to Lori, a vibrant, happy, helping flight attendant at Southwest. As I left the plane she handed me this note:

> "I smile because my loved ones and I have the gift of good health. I see many people, both young and elderly struggle because they aren't in the best health.

> "I smile, not only because I have a job in this uncertain economy, but because I have a job that I thoroughly enjoy.

> "I smile because I have a loving husband who makes me laugh, my children who are happy in their relationships and supportive of my choices in life, and loyal and caring friends.

> "I smile at other people because my smile may be the only smile they get all day!!"

§

Bekah, selling colorful fabric, had two nose pearls that were slightly repelling to me, but she had a smile that was a gentle welcome: "I really don't know. I just don't have it that bad."

§

Peter, with Porter Construction, said: "We're a friendly company."

§

Alison: "I'm getting a new mattress today, and I'm going back to Ellsberg Central for my GED." A mattress and a degree--an unexpected coupling of reasons, but certainly worth smiling about.

§

Lexi: "Oh man! Riding my quad. Being with friends and family and making other people happy."

§

Hanna, down in Ashford, Oregon, home of one of the Shakespearean Globe Theatres, said: "The nice people here." She described Ashford "as five square miles surrounded by reality." Because I write poetry, I smiled at the brilliant description!

§

Lorie, working at U-Haul in Tigard Oregon: "I help so many people here, and they are stressed in moving so I have to stay positive."

§

Two mothers pushing their babies in carriages, of course said: "Them." One mother added: "The sun."

§

Abbie, up on "Breadboard" overlooking Grizzly Mountain in Ashland: "My husband, Jeremy."

§

Dustin, in Council Bluffs, Iowa: "Music. And my partner lady."

§

Tracy in Iowa: "I just live life to the fullest. Life is just too short not to. I learned that now, and that helps me and everyone else."

§

Luke, the store manager at Firestone in Madison, Wisconsin: "Making people happy, and oh goodness, lots of things! Cars. My job."

§

Adam in Nebraska chuckled deeply when I asked him what put the smile on his face. Then, he lustily replied, "Life!"

§

A gentleman in big Springs, Nebraska simply gave me one word: "Sleep."

Rhonda replied: "I don't know." And then she added: "Dogs! Yeah. And grandkids."

§

China said, "Laughter. But sometimes not. When I have it, I do it."

§

Then Victor, her coworker in Bakersfield, California said one word: "Money." And then China laughed some more.

§

John, in a Loews in Wisconsin, had one of the warmest, brightest, un-asked-for greetings and he responded: "I like just getting up in the morning and seeing new people." The way I was greeted, he showed me he really does like meeting new people.

§

In Flagstaff, Arizona, with a vibrant voice, Zack said: "It's a good day!"

§

Sean in Albuquerque, New Mexico said: "Happy life. "

§

Moving on to the next state, in Kingman, Arizona Chris said: "I don't know. It's just a smile."

§

In a Quality Inn in Barstow, California, Christine said: "Every day I wake up, I'm happy."

§

Pauli, working at the *Flying J* in Big Springs, Nebraska, let out a litany of things that made her smile: "You know I have a lot to be thankful for: my three kids, my mom, my job, I get money, I get to make people's day better. Everything! There's always something to smile about."

§

Lorraine, in Barstow, California, said: "Just another day of working. I love working, because if I'm at home, I'd go crazy with my three kids. My aunt and uncle watch them for me."

§

Tall, blond, beautiful, but the smile outshone the beauty: Brandy. Working in Hale's restaurant in Hillsboro, Oregon, said: "I'm happy here. Life is too short to not smile." Food was good, and twice later I returned for more smiles.

§

Will, a guest at Hale's, overheard our conversation and volunteered: "This staff is great!"

He volunteered that he smiled because he was: "Hanging out with my son." He explained that he had a weekly lunch with his son Dave, who sat beside him.

I said I wished more dads would do that. Dave smiled.

§

So, I asked Dave about his smile, and I told him he couldn't return the favor and say, "His dad." So, he passed the compliment to Brandy saying: "Coming here and spending time with Brandy."

All that in a restaurant, where bread is the staff of life. Could it not also be that "Smiles are the stuff of life."

§

Lucia said: "I don't know, I'm always smiling." I said you've got to give me more than that. She reflected back the golden rule: "I like to be treated like I try to treat others."

§

I went to repair a zipper and met Mark who calls himself "Dr. Sole and Mr. Heel." He replied astoundingly: "I am a survivor of five heart attacks."

I had to ask him again to be sure I had heard him correctly. He explained that he had had three by-pass operations, one stent, and another unnamed heart attack. His smile was real and warm in the middle of a neat grey mustache that curled 270 degrees around his mouth. Five heart attacks and still working and shining smiles to us!

§

Veronica said: "It just comes naturally."

§

Gavin, one of the more efficient and friendly TV cable men from Frontier, said; "I enjoy making customers happy." I said: "Come on, that's your nice smile from your job; what else puts a smile on your face?" And he said: "Seriously, I enjoy fixing things. Problem-solving. It makes me happy."

§

Anon: "Just waking up every day. Not everyone can. I have. I'm lucky enough. And nothing can stop me unless I do it."

§

A woman jogger had a tee-shirt proclaiming: *Badass Mom.* She said: "I'm running! A great day!"

§

"Oh... my wife. And God is good," said Joshua.

§

Vanessa said, "My dog and my family."

§

"My smile? Ahhh...One hundred dollars." The first capitalistic response. And in America!

§

Andrea, selling solar cells in Oregon: "I'm drinking good coffee. I'm in the vegan capital of the US. Tattoos. And in believe in the good things."

§

Sabrina Leaf, in her mystical wonderful world of creative hand-molded earthenware, said with wide open arms and a smile to match: "All of this! This is like my happy spot!"

Sabrina sells her wizard pottery in the Portland Craft Market, which has more original artists, with more attractive creations than I have encountered elsewhere. I sent her my book, *The Wizard,* and she sent me one of her magical wizards who stands above me right now, smiling down--well at least he is looking down--sternly inspiring me and reminding me of Sabrina's smile.

§

Charlie stumped me: "Good veins put a smile on my face." Huh? "I'm an EMT." That put a smile on my face.

§

Brad, a check-out clerk at the very friendly local Trader's Joes, responded when I asked him whether he wanted me to swipe my card or use the chip. "And salsa?" he asked. It took me a few seconds to register, then Brad broke into a huge smile. He said humor helped him to smile. I might also enter his quote into a slowly growing collection of: *Quick Wit.* He'll get in two books with one comment and one huge smile!

§

Seage, serving Maca, a coffee-like drink, said: "Bats. They are so cute!"

§

Jamie, a big cuddly teddy bear of a man, simply said "Attention." I paused and then I understood it. Like everyone, he liked to be stroked and to be given attention.

§

Dustin in Council Bluffs, Iowa: "Music. And my partner lady."

§

Vanessa said, "My dog and my family."

§

Luke in Madison, Wisconsin: "Making people happy, and oh goodness, lots of things! Cars. My job."

§

Quinn, somewhere in the Pacific Northwest, said: "My marriage."

§

Stephanie, a TIAA rep talking on the phone, made me want to write another book: *What Puts the Lilt in your Voice?* She was trouble-shooting my password, and her voice was warm and friendly I told her I was going to put her in this book because I could "*hear*" the smile on her face. She is only one of two "smiles" in this book that I have not seen. The rest are visual, but I am a student of vocal tone which carries the real message, and which also carries the smiles.

§

A lady came out of Trader Joe's, saw me standing by the door way and just lit me up with a smile that long ago had fired and nestled in my heart. The lady was my wife.

§

"When my kids are asleep. I love to just look at their faces." Pat.

§

Arri, whose smile drew me to her, said: "I practice." She certainly had, for her smile had become part of her, telling me a lesson.

§

Estefania, working at the Green Festival in Portland, Oregon, said: "Just being here. This is a fun event." "Then she added: "And I just moved into a new house!"

§

Leah, working for Solar City, was enthusiastically telling me about Elon Musk who owned the company. As she beamed I asked her and she replied: "Making people smile." Instantly she turned the question back to me: "What makes you smile? "Just as fast I answered: "Right now, you."

§

Cathy Newton, who was selling total body vibrating machines, instantly said: "Jesus."

§

Marcus, at a Chevron station, was polite to an excess saying, "Sir this, sir that." (Oregon does not let consumers pump their own gas, and rarely do you get that friendly face that you got some thirty years ago smiling at you through your windshield while they cleaned it.) When Marcus came to my window and smiled, I asked, and he said: "Nice people, sir."

§

Danya, at a dental clinic: "Oh, I don't know." She paused: "Life is good."

§

Mariam, a young Asian woman, said "I'm sick, but I still try and smile."

§

Beth Anne, the oldest DQ clerk around, was whirling me up a chocolate malt when she also stirred my tummy with such a smile that I had to ask her. I received a witty, wonderful, instant response: "I turn into a butterfly, a monarch, in five minutes." After I laughed at her creative free-floating answer, Beth Anne put the chocolate in the malt: "And these kids here, the young people working with me, they put the smile on."

§

"It's a stunning day! And the power of the sea!" said the gentleman on an overlook of a promontory jutting ruggedly into the Pacific Ocean.

§

Samantha, at Freddy's: "Spending time with my great grandmother." I said: "Wow, what a lady." When Samantha saw how impressed I was that she got such joy from three generations above her, she noted that the younger people also lit up her smile: "I fall for the old Southern charm. I am going to South Carolina. I like guys with manners. After that, babies." A rich answer arising from creativity, charm, manners, and human connections--no wonder the smile.

§

Sarah Jane is so sweet! She just let me cut in line because I'm in a hurry. Her sweatshirt reads: *Love Cannon Beach*. Her one word response was: "Aster." When I raised my eyebrows she added: "She's my first baby, and I married the love of my life, and I would say that helps in a big way!"

§

Casi King who runs a huge glass repair company said: "Small children." She has the energy of a teenager herself, and the warm graciousness of a lady.

§

I met Jessica walking her daughter and front-packing her baby. I talked to her small daughter and as Jessica smiled I popped the question. Her single word answer: "Jesus!" Her tone was so enthusiastic, spontaneous, and loving that I said, "That sounds better than coffee." She replied that coffee is a close second as she laughed and her smile warmed some more.

§

Monica said, "My children." Then she laughed and brightened her smile as she added: "Food."

§

Anon: "Having a good day."

§

"My day is almost done," said a salesclerk at REI who did not want to be identified because her quote implied that her happiness to be done working for the day could be wrongly interpreted.

§

Megan gave me the most basic of life-affirming qualities that make people smile, such as the frequent response of: "Just happy to be alive." Megan said even more basically: "Breathing."

§

And another Anon: "Hanging out with friends."

§

Diomassi was in her first week as a vendor at a western airport: "I'm enjoying this."

§

An elderly gentleman listening to the fish-stacking interchange was smiling with enjoyment. I put my arm around his shoulder and said: "You've got a nice smile. I'm not age-discriminating here, but I must admit I'm a little prejudiced towards the ladies. But take a look at Susan's smile! I think you'll agree she's got us both beat." He smiled and nodded.

§

This is Jeffrey. He's a happy guy with his customers. He said, "Being alive." And he told me a story about a friend of his with a heart condition that put his own life in perspective.

§

This is Michaela and she said, "Helping others." Since she was working in a retail store and had to be friendly to customers I pushed her: "Is that a real, or a customer smile?" She responded and said: "Yes, this is me." Her co-worker next to her affirmed her answer.

"This is me!" What a wonderful solid self-affirmation that we all can smile from!

§

An intake employee at Kaiser dental has a great smile and he says he's always like that. He continues to smile while he searches for data in his computer.

§

"A lot of things actually. Life in general I guess." And Crystal's lovely smile is behind the counter at McDonald's in Baker City, Oregon.

§

This is Christy in Fred Meyers in Hillsboro,
Oregon. She is smiling gorgeously now as she
works in the furniture area. She's one of the more
helpful people I have run into and when I asked
her the question she said: "My kids." And then she
said: "I have six daughters."

And I'll bet a half dozen of them are smilers.

§

My son Scott and I were talking to Savannah who
was working at the Hops, a farm team in Hillsboro,
Oregon. She told us: "People close to you," as she
bashfully looked down with the slightest glance at
her co-worker. She had that knowing look that
said: you know whom I'm referring to.

§

Jessica, in Paradise Inn at Mt. Rainier Park, said:
"Sunshine. Friends. Nature."

§

Nelia, working at WinCo, a giant bulk supermarket in Oregon: "When I'm busy." Since I was the only one in the check-out line, she was not "busy" but she smiled. I wonder if I should come back and see if she smiles brighter when she has a long line?

§

Tracy, also working at WinCo gave me my sermon: "I count my blessings every day. God is good, and every day I read the King James Bible in the morning."

§

Alannah, working at Baby & Me, a children's consignment shop in Portland, Oregon: "I have a little brother. He always makes me smile."

§

Coleen, also at Baby & Me: "Most people. My son. Chocolate!" And then she laughed.

§

"Like, everyone needs it. You don't know when," said Julia working at Fresh Foods, a new neat food store across from *Mo's* in Cannon Beach, Oregon. Julia said she gives hugs too.

§

"I'm working," said Paola, also at Fresh Foods.

§

Someone in the Beaverton Farmers' Market: "I'm alive. And you've got to make a smile every day."

§

Somewhere in Wyoming or Idaho, words poured out of Laurie talking spontaneously and eloquently. I wish I had a picture of her expressive face that matched her words: "I think the smile on my face, real fast, comes from life. Life! Yes, that is good. Life is a gift. Yeah, I love it and take it as an adventure that we are just doing new and different things, that we're making known the unknown, then everyone is making all known their own."

Laurie is an art teacher at West High School, yet she could also thrive teaching English with her literary ability. Her laugh is contagious. Thank you, Laurie.

§

Teresa said: "Puppies." Surprisingly, that was only the second *puppy* that I had recorded. Then she said: "Making people happy, when you can really make a difference. I wake up every morning glad that the Lord lets me be alive."

§

From the Mile-High City comes welcoming warmth: "Friends. I do this for work all the time and just being with my friend. One of my favorite things to do in Denver is just have dinner parties with my friends, and everybody comes over and it's like why don't we do this every night?"

Lovely Rachel is speaking, and her response is so enthusiastic and open that I just want to kiss her. Well, that's a different book asking the question: *"May I kiss you?"*

§

I have Kayla here working at a toy store in Madison, Wisconsin. She gives credit to her mother for her smile: "First my parents put the smile on my face; everyone says I have my mother's smile." And then she said: "I like my job here."

§

Jose, a crewcut and happy twenty-year-old working at the Sinclair Station in Boardman Oregon, on August 21, 2016, gave us our daily mantra: "SMILE AT LIFE. That's my motto."

§

Jose's coworker, Dora, was smiling at our interchange and when I asked her she just reaffirmed Jose's answer and said: "Life, too." Just talking about smiles had made her smile.

§

Apryle in Idaho: "I woke up this morning." She had given her reason, a solid one. But when I waited for more she said: "A lot of people didn't." Her reason hit hard home.

§

The third time I ate lunch at Hales in Hillsboro, Oregon, Brandy was the waitress. She is close to the all-time high of smilers. She melts me when she smiles. For a second time I asked her, and she reminded me that she had told me on an earlier visit that life was too short not to smile.

Uh oh. I had better wrap this book up soon while I have a little memory working. And I will return to Hales again, not for their giant omelets or a cup of coffee, but for a cup of Brandy's smiles.

§

Michelle was at the post office in Hillsboro, Oregon picking up her mail since her mail box had been knocked down by a driver who took off. She said: "Nice weather." She added that: "The Federal fine for damaging and running is as high as 250 K and three years in jail." The hit-and-run mailbox flattener was caught. I could not tell if Michelle was secretly smiling at that, but I'll bet he's not smiling.

§

Kristin, at Mt. Rainier Lodge: "I love smiling, and looking at my friend, Amy. She dances."

§

Her friend, Amy, was across the hall in a gift shop wearing glasses with a basketball hoop attached to the front of the eye-glass rim. A small basketball dangled on a string. She dips her head and dangles the ball, then jerks her head to swing the ball up towards the hoop. While doing this Amy dances. Her friend across the hall smiles.

After two airballs, Amy said she likes to make people laugh while doing this dance with a straight face. Also, "Sunshine, and being up on Rainier!"

§

Ada: "When I see people happy."

§

Tilly, handing out coffee and smiles from a
drive-through window on Sunset Highway leading
to the fabulous Oregon coast said: "That's just how
I am every day." When I told her that there was a
lighthouse out in the Pacific about twenty miles
from her named *Terrible Tilly* she said: "I know.
That's what my mother calls me." We both laughed
as she revealed her full name was Matilda.

§

"I'm just happy. My tattoos make me happy
and then, when I found out I had a cousin working
here at the winery, I was happy. The universe
makes me happy when it brings people together."
All this from Denise, and her open
expansiveness and happy warm smiles make
seeing her, loving her.

§

Exiting the Post Office in Hillsboro I held the door for Pat, and her husband David followed. When I asked Pat about her smile David instantly, cheerily butted in and said: "I do." Then Pat said: "Life is too short not to smile at people." Their smiles and friendliness might have got them in trouble, for they invited me over, giving me phone and address. Since David had told me he had taught math, I told him he might be making a mistake trusting me because a mathematical person cannot read facial expressions very well. I can't remember if he laughed or began pushing his calculator buttons.

§

"Beautiful days," Sarah told me. "And small things like weather and rain, and when it's smoky then you lock the smoke out." [There were multiple forest fires burning in Oregon.] "And my colleagues here at work, like Sharon."

§

"I've always been that way, but I was sad when I was young," said Michelle. "It was one of my aunts who told me that when you grow up you're going to always have wrinkles. You have a choice whether you have smile or frown lines?"

§

This is Brett, serving sample food at Trader Joes. He's about 64, hair combed back, and with a smile that caused me to ask him what was in the food he was serving. He said: "I have the cans of dog food back behind the counter." He told me he likes making people smile with his humor!

§

"Oh, my wife and God is good," said Joshua.

§

"Okay," Richard said. "I'm alive. I like helping people." Richard was in a Home Depot. When he saw me with arms full he said: "You need a basket."

When I found out that Richard did not even work there, I knew the guy really does enjoy helping people. A friend is moving out down the street. I wish I had Richard's address, because he would make a great neighbor.

§

Melissa: "Honesty." An unusual response. Abstract concepts like truth, honesty, and goodness rarely burst into smiles. But as long as Melissa broached the subject, I think all of these answers from smilers were basically honest, though at times I could see embarrassment, and of course, some concealment. Perhaps smilers are honest because that is their nature, perhaps because they were thinking about positive things which they had no need to cover with a lie.

§

Tracy in Iowa: "I just live life to the fullest. Life is just too short not to. I learned that smiling helps me and everyone else."

§

I was so blown away with this next waterfalling response that I missed the first name. Sorry.

"We all get a little life, and some of us a little less, but it's all how we use what we have. We make it brighter or we make a mess, but in America we're raised to live alone, to be there and rugged, to go out and homestead. Instead our lives aren't showing that we are all one, and will need each other to raise each other's awareness. And yes, you do take care of your brother, yes your sister is your sister."

Wow! I feel humbled. I apologize again for missing the name.

§

I know I have forgotten to record many smiles that were given to me in passing. If I end up compiling a third volume because I can't break this habit of asking, I will record more carefully.

I think it is fitting that I end with a list sent to me by Shanté. Perhaps it contains some of the reasons behind the smiles that slipped by me.

"Hi Gary, this is Shanté from Best Buy. Things that make me smile:

- People that are happy. It's nice to see other people enjoying life.
- Babies. They are just so cute and innocent.
- Confidence. Everyone should be happy with who they are.
- God. When I'm in a bad mood, I know he is there for me and wouldn't put me through anything I can't handle. When I'm in a good mood, I am thankful for what I have.

- Music. With all the different types of music
  I listen to, I feel great.
- Dancing. It makes me feel free and I can
  express myself.
- Family time. I am forever grateful to have
  time to be with family.
- Good deeds. I love when people are honest
  and do helpful things not for themselves, but
  for others.
- Jokes. They are funny.
- Being complimented. Everyone likes that.
- Making other people happy."

Wow! I'll bet you can find a few familiar favorites
from that list. Thanks Shanté!

Reflections

Is there a common theme behind all these smiles? Their responses, except for the short ones of one word, are all different; but I think there is an underlying feeling of gratefulness that supports these smiles. The smilers seem to accept their lives and appreciate it. They seem to look at what they have, not at what they do not have. And for many of them what they do have, and what they emphasize, is people, nature, and simply life!

Perhaps surprising to many Americans who are fully engaged in our capitalistic system, *things* are not mentioned that often. Early I recorded one smiler who said: "My phone," and I expected others but few came. Things seem to be a small source of happiness. Studies of individuals and nations have shown that beyond the basics of survival and comfort, *things* do not add to the happiness quotient. (We might now have to add a smart phone to the basics of survival.)

Personally, I experienced how limited things are to our happiness when I was skimming a book called *14,000 Things to be Happy About.* 14,000 items! In comparison, this book in your hand begins to appear puny. But when I read some of the 14,000 items, I found only three or four that began to light my mind; however, those few did not actually put a smile on my face. I am sure I was biased, but I realized there was a great difference in receiving the smiles directly from a happy face and in looking at a list of words that appeared to be easily gathered from a dictionary. I agree with the implied premise of *14,000,* that almost everything in the universe is worth being happy about, but as mentioned, I found very few times that the smilers themselves named *things.*

Perhaps the most frequent response (and perhaps the most profound) is: *Life,* usually said with enthusiasm. *I'm alive!* This response is more frequent from the older smilers. Many say they are "natural" smilers who just are that way, or that it is genetic. There are a few who have learned to smile through practice and are now smilers. It is a rewarding pleasure to hear them explain how they became who they are. There are those people who appreciate all the gifts of just being, and they show that in their smiles. Some of them name some of the sources of their smiles: their children, spouses, friends, nature, or their jobs.

Perhaps the most inspiring smilers are those who smile in adversity like Miriam who said, "I'm sick, but I still try and smile." And even more uplifting are the few who smile not just in, but from adversity: do you remember Ellie who said: "I have a chronic disease that has helped me to think positively. I expect everything to go the worst possible way, and even if it is bad, then it is not as bad as I imagined!"

I am still in awe of that humbling meeting with Ellie.

Just as a quirkish thought: I wonder what would happen if I asked a reverse question to those people who drooped or displayed a glowering face, a question such as: "What makes you sad?" or "What puts that sour look on your face?" Do you think I would get any answers? Or perhaps a: "Mind you own business." Or worse.

Philosophers have reflected directly on happiness at least since Aristotle's *Nicomachean Ethics*. My own formula is

$$H = K \Rightarrow A + A$$

*Happiness is Knowledge into Action
then Accepting the results*

More simply, do what is right. More elaborately, live trying to learn and know and then act accordingly. When we choose honestly and then act, we have done the best we can, and when we repeat that action we begin to build a habit. And habit builds character. And a person of character is someone who both accepts the results of their efforts or fate, and accepts who they are, and yet is striving to learn more and live accordingly. Okay, back to the simple $h = k \Rightarrow a + a$.

Smiles then are an indicator of happiness. Often smiles grace the faces of people who have reached an understanding, acceptance, and gratefulness about their lives. These smiles are illuminated by real people with reasons and feelings behind their smiles which brighten our days. As the recipient of these smiles, I have been rainbowed in human wonder and warmth and joy, and I hope some of their smiles have filtered through their words to you.

Afterglow

Quite often the afterglow of a sunset spreads wider and leaves me fuller of warmth and beauty. Upon departing the smilers I carry that warmer feeling with me. Some of their smiles stay in memory for life. I am sure all of them have changed me in some way, adding to my positive hopeful view of humanity.

Wow! A smile! The power! The gift! The small cost! The large reward to the receiver--and the giver!

Any doubt about?

And I am grateful. Thank you, thank you for your smiles!

§

you walked thru my life
in a magic once only moment
we kissed smiles
and I hope the kiss lit your soul
and left a glow that clings to you
for the rest of your life

thirty feet above me
you glance down and smile
disappearing down a glass walkway

too far to leap and follow
I lift my head
and thank your sparkling smile
and swear I'll greet each smile
as spring on a new born planet

smile!